Managing Compliance

Sven Kette is a Senior Assistant in the Seminar for Sociology at the University of Lucerne. He researches and teaches there in the "Organization and Knowledge" Working Group. His work focuses on organizational theory and research on companies.

Other Books by Sven Kette

Kette, Sven (2018): Unternehmen. Eine sehr kurze Einführung. Springer VS (*Business Firms. A Very Brief Introduction*; currently available only in German).

Sebastian Barnutz is a partner and senior consultant at Metaplan, a company that specializes in strategic consulting and organizational development. He consults in particular the pharmaceutical sector, medical technology firms, and the energy sector.

To contact us:
Metaplan
Goethestraße 16
D-25451 Quickborn
Germany
Phone: +49 41 06 61 70
info@organizationaldialoguepress.com
www.metaplan.com

Sven Kette
Sebastian Barnutz

Managing Compliance

A Very Brief Introduction

Organizational Dialogue Press
Princeton, Hamburg, Shanghai, Singapore, Versailles, Zurich

ISBN (Print) 978-1-7323861-8-1
ISBN (EPUB) 978-1-7323861-9-8

Copyright © 2019 by Sven Kette, Sebastian Barnutz

All rights reserved. No part of this publication may be reproduced or transmitted in any form or by any means, without permission in writing from the author.

Translated by: Lee Holt
Cover Design: Guido Klütsch
Typesetting: Thomas Auer
Project Management: Tabea Koepp
www.organizationaldialoguepress.com

Contents

Preface: Managing Compliance Beyond the Machine Model of Organizations 7

1.
What is Compliance Management? A Proposed Definition and Classification Informed by Organizational Theory 12

    1.1 Compliance Management—A Definition 14
    1.2 Compliance Management and
        the Three Sides of Organizations 21

2.
The Temptations and Limits of an Instrumental-Rational Approach 28

    2.1 The Panoptic Dream of Total Control 29
    2.2 The Function of Control Fictions 33
    2.3 The Shortsightedness of Panoptic Control Visions and
        the Significance of Informal Latitude 38

3.
Managing Compliance Management—Approaches to Designing Compliance Management 44

    3.1 Beyond Total Control, or the Art of Avoiding Awareness 48

    3.2 Beyond Unconditional Sanctioning,
         or the Composure to Maintain Informalities 52

    3.3 Beyond the Limits of Formalization,
         or the Danger of Overlooking Organizational Risks 58

4.
Discursive Compliance Management—Conclusion 63

Bibliography 69

Preface: Managing Compliance Beyond the Machine Model of Organizations

Rules have always played an important role in and for companies, administrations, hospitals, schools and universities. Recently, however, ensuring compliance with rules—whether legal regulations, voluntary codes of ethics or internal organizational requirements—has come to be seen as an independent success factor for organizational action. And violating these rules seems to pose a risk. This discussion takes place under the heading of 'compliance management,' which refers to organizational processes and structures intended to ensure compliance with existing rules and the creation of new rules as necessary. Such compliance management procedures are particularly important against the background of major economic and corruption scandals, which regularly raise the question of liability. In the most prominent cases—Enron, Siemens or Volkswagen—the failure of organizational compliance management was not the sole cause of the breaches of rules. In the aftermath of these scandals, one of the main consequences was compliance management reform (Barreveld 2002; Fusaro/Miller 2002; Nelson 2017; Salter 2008; Weidenfeld 2011). The boom in the topic of compliance may also stem from the fact that the establishment of compliance procedures is frequently an indispensable prerequisite for the formation of business partnerships. This may be because compliance is a requirement for participating in public tenders, or because compliance requires that business partners may only enter into business relationships with companies that conduct compliance management.

At first glance, this increased orientation toward rules may seem understandable, or even welcome. After all, the economic damage caused by corruption, cartel formation or other financial crimes is not insignificant. However, it is also clear that ensuring employees behave in accordance with the rules is no trivial undertaking. We often hear complaints about 'elaborate' or even 'nonsensical' compliance regulations and the additional effort associated with them. The crucial questions, however, are these: What is changing in and for companies as a result of the introduction of compliance management procedures? What are the central areas of conflict in the design of compliance management? And finally: What levers can be used in the design of compliance management and the handling of central areas of conflict? Answering these questions first requires an in-depth analysis of the effectiveness of organizational compliance management.

The aim of this book is to enable readers to recognize, precisely and comprehensively, the operating principles of compliance management and its effects on organizations, and to identify starting points for the design of a compliance management regime. Such an analytical view of the functioning of organizational compliance management is often obscured by normative and rationalistic perspectives. There are two reasons for this: first, because people are interested in how things *should be* from a normative perspective, or, second, because people are attached to a highly simplified rationalistic notion of organizations that underestimates complex inner-organizational dynamics and overestimates the chances of success for planning activities.

Working from a foundation of normative and rationalistic assumptions, the discussion to date has emphasized the need to ensure compliance with the rules or—wherever this is not possible—to at least record and sanction rule deviations as completely as possible. We often overlook the fact that deviations from the rules can be functional for organizations and that the procedures for ensuring compliance—regardless of their success—can themselves have dysfunctional effects. Chapter 1 first develops an understanding of the organization that takes these considerations into account and classifies compliance management accordingly. This provides the foundation for avoiding a common error, namely, understanding organizations as systems that, like machines, can be completely pre-planned and controlled by means of formally defined rules (Chapter 2). Building on these insights, we will show in Chapter 3 that the organizational design challenge consists of managing compliance management yourself. Instead of setting up a single department responsible for monitoring compliance and sanctioning infringements, it is important to integrate this department into organizational structures in such a way that the compliance management department itself does not become harmful. In conclusion, we argue that organizational structures should be designed in such a way that compliance management and specialist departments can reach a discursive agreement on the intentions of the rules and the consequences of each specific regulatory arrangement (Chapter 4).

The approach we present here for managing compliance management is based on several years of experiences in working with companies, ministries, administrations, armed forces, police forces, universities, schools, hospitals and non-profit organizations. Even though this book results from practical work and is aimed primarily at practitioners in organizations, we maintain that our approach is aligned with the insights gleaned from the latest approaches to organizational theory.

We believe that organizational theoreticians and organizational practitioners have fundamentally different quality criteria. The assumption that "good science" necessarily leads to "good practice" is naive because the criteria that scholars use to define success are so different from those of practitioners. Yet despite this difference, which we believe is insuperable, our aspiration here is to present a proven approach in such a way that organizational scholars cannot dismiss it right away as uninteresting. And even if this slim volume is written primarily for practitioners, attentive organizational scholars may also find one or the other interesting theoretical innovation.

This book is part of the *Management Compact* series in which we present the essentials for the management of organizations in the context of modern organizational theories. In addition to this volume, *Managing Compliance*, the series includes books on the subjects of *Designing Organizations, Managing Projects, Developing Strategies, Developing Mission Statements,* and *Influencing Organizational Culture*. In our book, *Lateral Leading*, we assess how power, understanding and trust influence the management of organizations. Because these books are all based on the same understanding of organizations, attentive readers will notice related trains of thought and similar formulations in all of the volumes in this series. These overlaps were created intentionally to emphasize the unity of the ideas behind the series and to highlight the connections between the volumes. You can read more about the theoretical foundations of organizations in *Organizations: A Systems Approach* (Kühl 2013) and *Unternehmen: Eine sehr kurze Einführung (Business Firms: A Very Brief Introduction;* currently available only in German) (Kette 2018a).

We do not believe in "simplifying" texts for managers and consultants by crowding our texts with bullet points, executive summaries, graphical presentations of how the text flows, or exercises. The *Management Compact* series presents brief books that enable readers to understand the central ideas without these kinds of aids. That is why in this book, and in all of the other *Management Compact* volumes, we are very sparing with the use of visual aids. Along with a very limited number of diagrams, there is only one element that makes reading easier: small boxes. We use these to present examples that illustrate our ideas, or to mark productive connections to organizational theory. Readers who are short on time or are not interested in these aspects can skip over the text boxes without losing the thread.

This book was developed in the Metaplan training program, "Management and Consulting in Discourse." We would also like to thank the participants over the years for their many tips and ideas as well as the members of the "Quickborner Kreis."

1. What is Compliance Management? A Proposed Definition and Classification Informed by Organizational Theory

For several years now, compliance management has been one of the boom topics in management discourse. This is not just another buzzword that everyone who wants to appear competent needs to know; the term may be used in purely rhetorical ways, too. However, compliance management gains its importance—and risk—precisely where it is not merely paying lip service, but where organizational structures are also being redesigned in accordance with its principles. This happens above all in corporate contexts, especially in the financial and pharmaceutical sectors. However, compliance management is also gaining prominence in other types of organizations, whether in hospitals, public administrations or even non-profit organizations (Silverman 2008).

The term "compliance" comes from the English language and means adherence, observance, or alignment, referring to adherence to, observance of, or alignment with rules. These include both legal regulations and voluntary codes and standards to which an organization is committed, as well as internal rules within the organization. The thematic breadth of these rules is broad, ranging from corruption prevention to antitrust issues and initiatives against money laundering, to data protection and environmental protection measures. Compliance management has the task of enabling employees to act in accordance with all of these external and internal requirements—and to ensure that they do so.

Despite overt efforts to systematically compile various compliance management instruments (for example ISO 2014), there is no uniform compliance management concept at this time. Instead, there is a considerable range of (partial) concepts in the literature, which above all makes it clear that ultimately every organization must strive to find its own appropriate compliance management structures. For example, there is a large number of manuals and practical guides on the topic that are difficult to keep track of; they often proceed from similar diagnoses, but in some cases differ considerably in terms of instruments and priorities (Singh/Bussen 2015; Steinberg 2011). A large part of these texts focuses mostly on legal aspects regarding the question of whether there is a legal obligation to introduce compliance management, and which elements should be included in compliance management. Such discussions therefore focus on legal texts and examples of best practices. The urgency of the issue is usually ascertained by referencing the imminent legal and reputational risks that could arise if employees break the rules. In addition, compliance management is recommended as a tool in the context of sustainability, quality management, digitization and many other fields. Compliance management can help if there is a risk that employees will pursue the interests of their own specialist department too narrowly. And in situations where work is carried out under the pressures of success and time, the incentives to sugarcoat emission values, skip over safety concerns and make agreements with competitors are so great that compliance management is needed in order to avoid costly readjustments down the line.

Even with the wide range of concepts and tools for designing organizational compliance management, we can still identify three core problems that are regularly assigned to compliance management. First, compliance management should *monitor compliance*, whether through active monitoring or by passively accepting reports of violations; second, compliance management should *sanction any deviations*; and third, compliance management should *develop rules*, whether this means adapting existing rules or developing new rules within the organization, or transforming external standards and laws into internal rules within the organization.

According to this logic, compliance management appears to be the solution to the problem of avoiding rule-breaking behavior. Most of the time, however, this does not take into account the problems caused by the introduction of compliance management. These problems come into view when a more fundamental approach is taken and when the introduction and design of organizational compliance management are discussed against the background of a theoretically informed understanding of organizations. Now we will locate compliance management within an overarching framework of organizational theory and suggest a more precise definition.

1.1 Compliance Management—A Definition

From the systems theoretical perspective of organizational research, compliance management is the *centralization of rule monitoring* within an organization. In organizations that do not have compliance management, rule monitoring authority is distributed across the entire organization. Whether violations of the rules are generously overlooked or whether even minor details are used as grounds for deterrent punishments is largely the responsibility of the respective (intermediate) supervisors. Some of these individuals have considerable scope for interpretation, which can result in a rather inconsistent landscape of compliance management efforts; for example, one department may maintain a slush fund while another department bills even the smallest expenses in strict accordance with the regulations.

The introduction of compliance management changes this by assigning the responsibility for rule monitoring to a specific unit. Although this does not exempt supervisors from their compliance-related responsibilities, it does limit their scope for granting exceptions. The boss who prefers to turn a blind eye now finds himself compelled by compliance management to inflict punishments—and if he decides against this punishment, he may have to answer for it. Overlooking rule violations among employees then becomes a rule violation by the boss that is subject to sanctions. We can gain a more nuanced understanding of this situation and, above all, its consequences, by taking a closer look at organizational structure.

In the most general sense, the establishment of compliance management always means the establishment of one or several new positions. In organizational theory organizational units are understood as a bundle of three decision premises: the *communication channels*, which provide information about the relationship of one position to all other positions; the *decision programs*, which provide orientation with regard to the decisions to be taken; and the *personnel*, meaning the actual decision makers who hold a position. In this context, positions are the nodes of the organizational structure (Luhmann 2009; Luhmann 2018, 181-272; see also Kühl/Muster 2018 for a quick introduction).

The significance and effects of compliance management in a specific organization depend above all on how the compliance management position(s) are integrated into organizational communication channels, which decision rules apply to compliance management employees (decision programs), and the people who fill the positions. We will take a closer look at all three aspects below.

The Integration of Compliance Management into Organizational Communication Channels

Communication channels are a structural element of organizations that provide information on decision-making responsibilities and competences. The questions here are as follows: Who has to decide what exactly? Who should be consulted prior to certain decisions? To whom should certain decisions be reported? References to the communication channels of an organization can be found above all in the organization chart, which depicts the departmental and hierarchical structure. Rights of co-determination can also be understood as communication channels in this sense.

Although compliance management is not a copyrighted term and the specific arrangement of compliance management can turn out very differently in practice, using the term compliance management only appears meaningful if appropriate positions are also set up and integrated into the organizational communication channels. In the most economical case, this can result in a Compliance Officer. In this model, compliance tasks are assigned as additional tasks to an existing employee, without creating a fully separate position and hiring someone for it. In the larger scale version, an entire compliance department is created, headed by a Chief Compliance Officer, who may also be part of the company's Board of Management. Practically everything in between is conceivable. Just as the size of the departments and the hierarchical position can vary considerably from organization to organization, the same applies to the reporting channels. The ways in which compliance management must be informed about rule violations (e.g. via whistleblower hotlines), to whom compliance management must report observed rule violations (e.g. when is the Board of Management to be informed?) and who is to be involved in decisions regarding sanctions, are all questions for which there is no general answer. However, the need to clarify these issues represents one of the central challenges in designing compliance management. But no matter which variant an organization chooses, it is always a matter of naming responsibilities and defining decision-making powers.

The Programmatic Character of Compliance Management

The question of *who* has to make a decision does not yet provide information about *how* someone has to decide—or what he has to take into account when making his decisions. Organizations use *decision programs* to provide this orientation; these provide rules for decision making. They can, in the case of so-called purpose programs, set objectives and leave the choice of resources relatively open: "Increase your annual turnover by four percent!" Or, in the case of conditional programs, decision programs can be structured according to the if-then principle. This determines which conditions should lead to which decision consequences: *if* the order value is over 3,000 euros, *then* a two percent discount must be granted. In the context of compliance management, decision programs are relevant in at least three areas: rule monitoring, deviation sanctioning and rule development.

Rule monitoring programs. One of the central tasks of compliance management is to monitor compliance with rules in order to uncover violations. Decision programs structure this 'detective work' in fundamental ways, establishing what constitutes an occasion for an audit, setting audit rhythms, providing audit formats and the like.

Deviation sanctioning programs. A second program type that structures compliance management work concerns questions of sanctioning deviations from the rules. These include, for example, penalty catalogs that can more or less clearly specify how certain types of rule breaches are to be punished and what evidentiary requirements must be met in order for appropriate sanctions to be imposed.

Rule development programs. This third type of program is often overlooked in the discussion about compliance management. It directs attention to the fact that compliance management itself contributes to the creation of new rules in organizations, for example, if compliance management provides tools that help employees decide whether they can accept or issue business invitations. Once again, compliance management decision programs shape the framework within which such rule developments run their course. And even if the rules developed by compliance management only become valid upon their ratification at higher hierarchical levels, it is still clear that the decision to establish compliance management is at the same time a decision for the continuous development of new rules. And these new rules are less important for compliance management itself than for the departments that have to follow the rules, because these new rules will change the ways of working there.

At the same time, it is also true that decision programs can be designed differently and thus influence both the way in which compliance management is integrated and its organizational weight. For example, is there a plan for compliance management to support and accompany a specialist department in the independent formulation of rules, or can compliance management lay down directive rules for a specialist department? Does the monitoring of rule compliance tend to follow purpose programs or a conditional program logic?

Compliance Management Personnel

Personnel are the third structure-producing element in organizations. The mere definition of communication channels and decision programs has no consequences as long as the relevant position has not been filled with personnel who actually make decisions. As an organizational structure element, we should understand personnel as different people making different decisions. Despite all the orientation that communication channels and, above all, decision programs can provide, each specific decision-making situation also has a degree of openness to interpretation (Daft/Weick 1984; Weick et al. 2005; Kühl 2017b). Given this necessity of interpreting situations, it may make a difference whether a lawyer, a sociologist, a business economist or an engineer fills the corresponding position, since professional training privileges different techniques and instruments for interpreting situations.

Such necessities of situational interpretation can also be found in dealing with rules. This is obvious when it comes to creating new rules. However, the application of existing rules also always requires the assessment of specific individual cases in the light of more or less abstract rules (March 1994, 57ff.). The challenge for compliance management here is the same as for a soccer referee: the rule that a handball in the penalty box leads to a penalty kick is clear. And yet every call is subject to subtle interpretation, as is clear from weekly discussions about supposedly wrong decisions by referees.

Because lawyers are regarded as experts on rules and their interpretation, it is not surprising that they are the most frequent occupants of compliance management positions. Also, lawyers are most likely to understand the relevant legal regulations and to be able to check organizational circumstances for corresponding deviations. Compliance management is therefore often directly assigned to the legal department. Nonetheless, there is a growing range of qualification formats and continuing education courses aimed at training non-lawyers for compliance management tasks. The question of which qualification profile is preferred for compliance management positions is thus also a question related to the structure of organizational compliance management.

1.2 Compliance Management and the Three Sides of Organizations

In principle, we should be surprised that organizations are introducing compliance management at all. After all, organizations have always had to comply with laws. The formulation of internal rules is also an integral part of what constitutes organizations. An organization without any rules is simply not a formal organization (Ahrne/Brunsson 2011). Organizations not only have a particular tendency to establish rules; they also have specific mechanisms to protect these rules. Unlike families, for example, where rule violations usually lead to conflict and/or frustration, organizations are in a position to part with their members if they do not recognize the formal rules, or even violate them (Kühl 2015). But if organizations have always established rules and have also always been able to sanction violations sharply, what does compliance management add, and to what extent does it possibly even change the rules of the game? In order to understand organizational compliance management more precisely, it is necessary to systematically separate three sides of the organization: the formal side, the informal side and the display side of an organization (Kühl 2013, 138ff. for details; Kette 2018a, 49ff. especially with regard to business firms).

The *formal side* is about an organization's official body of rules. This includes the recognition of the communication channels listed in the organization chart as well as the decision programs described in process manuals, job descriptions and similar documents. Such formal expectations have thus always been designed to provide orientation and enable internal coordination within the organization, be it with regard to the flow of information or the making of decisions. However, formal expectations are not only (relatively) specific; they are also characterized by the fact that their recognition is made a condition for remaining in the organization. In other words, those who violate formal expectations always risk being expelled (Luhmann 1964).

Expectations on the *informal side* also have coordinating and decision-preparing functions. In many respects, these informal expectations are similar to those we know from our families or friends. They do not arise from a specific decision, nor can they be changed by means of a decision. Instead, they gradually evolve over time, when certain actions and behaviors are repeated so often that they eventually become expected and corresponding behavior is considered due. The fact that, for example, a travel application is not submitted until after the end of the trip may violate the formal expectation that travel applications must be submitted two weeks before the start of the trip. However, if this violation goes unpunished and the backdating of such after-the-fact travel requests is repeatedly accepted, an informal expectation may emerge that travel requests can be submitted later without any problems. But precisely because informal expectations are not officially decided on, their violation cannot be sanctioned—at least not officially—by a termination of membership. Instead, more subtle sanction mechanisms are put to work, such as the withdrawal of collegial support or even bullying.

Finally, the *display side of* an organization includes all of those texts and behaviors that are explicitly directed at customers, suppliers, investors, non-governmental organizations and many other audiences. They are intended to present the organization

What is Compliance Management? **23**

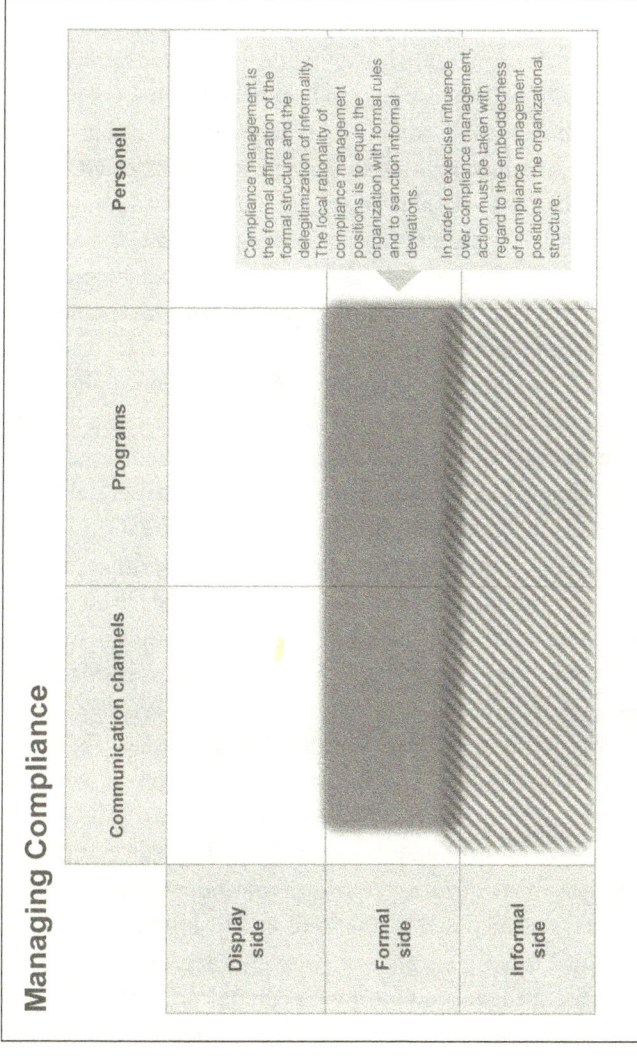

Diagram 1: Structure Matrix for Analyzing Organizations—Compliance Management as Meta-Formality

in a good light, as beautified façades. To this end, a whole series of social values are regularly woven into display side formulations that emphasize the modernity and rationality of the organization, but also document its conformity with general cultural principles (such as sustainability) (Brunsson 1989; Meyer/Rowan 1977). Such values are very abstract expectations that, although they offer hardly any direct orientation in specific decision-making situations, are nevertheless taken up in the external representation of organizations in order to gain external acceptance and legitimacy (Suchman 1995).

Only if we keep the three sides of the organization in mind, can we avoid two fundamental errors that are found again and again in practice and the discussion around the formation of organizational compliance management. The first mistake is to understand, whether explicitly or implicitly, the introduction of compliance management as an activity on the display side of the organization. One may find such display side management morally questionable, and even organization members may not let themselves be blinded by such smoke and mirrors (MacLean/Behnam 2010). However, such symbolic politics becomes a problem for organizations, mainly because it regularly fails. The reason for introducing compliance management, for example, may stem solely from the need to symbolically take external expectations into account. However, it is extremely unlikely that compliance management can be trimmed down to window dressing, with a purely symbolic function. On the contrary, findings from organizational research suggest that as soon as appropriate positions are established and equipped with competencies, they will also be heard within the organization (Hasse/Japp 1997; Kette 2019).

The second mistake is to overlook the effects of compliance management on the informal side. The introduction of compliance management expresses a particular intolerance towards the violation of formal expectations and thus towards informal practices. At least those formal expectations that are the subject of compliance management are particularly strengthened as a result. In this sense, compliance management is the formal affirmation of (parts of) the formal structure: from now on, we'll do everything by the book! Compliance management thus functions as a *meta-formality* (Kette 2017; Kette 2018b). However, compliance management does not only strengthen the formal structure that already exists; it also delegitimizes informal practices. To the extent that compliance management deals exclusively with explicitly formulated rules, it *cannot* recognize informal practices.

Whenever informal behaviors come to the attention of compliance management, this gives rise to formalization needs—in the logic of compliance management—in order to have clear rules available in the future. Compliance management formalizes a certain interpretation or situational interpretation and thereby delegitimizes others. The hope behind this is to make compliance with a superordinate standard transparent and verifiable by programming detailed if-then sequences. Compliance management thus unfolds a formalization dynamic in the form of conditional programs, which results in the increasing restriction of informal leeway.

The introduction of compliance management always means changing the relationship between the formal, the informal and the display side. Accordingly, the challenge is to keep all three sides in mind when introducing and designing compliance management, especially the effects on informal expectations and practices. It is precisely this aspect that is often neglected in rational approaches.

THEORY

Compliance Management as an Organizational Unit and as an Organizational Function

We have to distinguish between two perspectives in the analysis and design of compliance management: compliance management as an organizational unit and as an organizational function. Although both perspectives refer to each other, they each address different problems.

A perspective that focuses on *compliance management as an organizational unit* is interested in the question of which organizational units are entrusted with compliance management. Obviously, a whole range of design options is possible, and they all actually occur: organizations can appoint a Compliance Officer, they can set up a compliance management department, or they can assign compliance management tasks to existing organizational units, such as a legal department. In individual cases, such questions of allocation can have far-reaching consequences, not, however, on the basis of concrete job titles, but on the basis of the communication channels and decision programs defined as relevant for compliance management.

Compliance management, however, does not only refer to one (or more) organizational unit(s), but also to an *organizational function*. This perspective draws attention to the functions and effects of meta-formalization and the establishment of rule monitoring procedures, regardless of how such bodies are specifically designated in the respective organizations. From this perspective it becomes clear that meta-formalizations also occur in such organizations and may play a role that does not use the term 'compliance management' at all. The only questions are whether the organization in question has appropriate decision programs for rule monitoring, deviation sanctioning and rule development; the organization has established compliance management functions in this sense, and the communication channels have been defined in this context. On the other hand this perspective also sensitizes us to the fact that organizations can decide to go for a more or less comprehensive compliance management, depending on whether the meta-formalization refers to only a small range of the formal structure, or whether broad parts of the formal structure are subject to meta-formalization.

2. The Temptations and Limits of an Instrumental-Rational Approach

All employees should behave in accordance with the applicable rules; this is the basic tenor of the practical literature on compliance management. At the very least, the organizational rules would have to articulate applicable legal regulations and legally non-binding standards in a way that minimizes legal risks and reputational risks to the organization. Training courses and online tutorials are assumed to be an important instrument for reaching this goal. They are intended to make the rules known within the organization and to sensitize people to their observance. At the same time, however, such mandatory compliance training also serves as a kind of insurance policy for the organization and top management: If there are deviations from the rules, at least no employee can say they didn't know the rules.

However, while it is important to inform employees about relevant regulations, it is also important to obtain information about rule violations. In the debate about compliance management, consistent rule monitoring is thus the second cornerstone for ensuring that employees behave in accordance with the rules. Such monitoring can take various forms, ranging from mandatory data entry fields and automatically generated timestamps in digital input forms, to whistleblower hotlines.

If rule deviations are observed, the sanction of the deviating behavior represents the third pillar for ensuring rule-compliant behavior. These can range from retraining to job loss. The certainty that control deviations are detected—and punished—should have a deterrent effect and thus increase compliance with the rules.

2.1 The Panoptic Dream of Total Control

The idea of setting up compliance management as an organizational unit that overlooks the entire organization and can control the behavior of all employees is very similar to the panoptic prison. The concept of the panoptic prison, conceived by the British philosopher Jeremy Bentham (2017) at the end of the eighteenth century and made famous by the works of Michel Foucault (1979), describes a penitentiary in which all prison cells are arranged in a multi-storey ring construction. In the center of the inner courtyard of this ring building there stands a watchtower from which all prison cells can be seen. But because the prisoners cannot see into the watchtower, they remain uncertain about the direction in which the prison guards are looking. This leads the inmates to discipline themselves. If we extend this logic to its furthest conclusion, there would be no need for actual monitoring at all, and the watchtower could remain unmanned.

Although compliance management does not aim to replace actual monitoring with self-discipline of employees, a panoptic view of the organization is exactly what compliance management aims to achieve: the behavior of the employees should be made transparent and verifiable, so that violations of the rules can be detected. And because all employees know about it, such deviations from the rules should not occur in the first place.

This approach to ensuring rule-compliant behavior on the part of organizational members is ultimately a revival of old optimism about control. This is based on the idea that the behavior of the organization's members could be controlled quite well if they were only monitored and controlled closely and consistently enough. This idea is as old as organizational research itself. It originates from an idea that today is called the "instrumental-rational machine model" of the organization and was most impressively formulated by Max Weber (2009 [1972], 551ff.). According to Weber, organizations formulate an overall purpose, for the achievement of which partial purposes are formulated, which in turn—in the form of task descriptions—are assigned to individual offices or departments. The result is an understanding of organizations as a perfect machine in which one cogwheel meshes seamlessly with the other. "Scientific Management," developed and propagated by Frederick Taylor (1967), is very similar to Weber's descriptions and is also based on a mechanistic idea of organization. At the beginning of the twentieth century, Taylor wanted to optimize the work and even movement sequences of workers through detailed time and movement studies, so that these tasks could be carried out with maximum efficiency. This approach also issues from the idea that an organization can be coordinated exclusively through its formal side of explicitly formulated rules.

As a result, the model of organizations as machines was often criticized as too simplistic and unrealistic. Organizational research provided important insights into the development of more complex ideas about the internal functioning of organizations. Above all, we should mention the discovery of informal structures. After the famous "Hawthorne studies" (Mayo 1966 [1933]; Roethlisberger et al. 1967 [1939]) recognized the importance of personal relationships and informal structures, interest was initially focused on instrumentalization by management. Soon, however, the informal side of organizations became an important object of analytically oriented organizational research (Gouldner 1964 [1954]) and the starting point of modern organizational sociology.

But even within the more practically oriented management discourse, more and more such ideas were gaining prominence, questioning and watering down the image of organizations as perfect machines. What was viewed as needed instead were "post-bureaucratic companies" (Heckscher/Donnellon 1994) and "agile forms of organization" (Robertson 2015), which were more committed to "self-organization" and dispensed with overly strict top-down planning in favour of "semi-autonomous production groups" and a corresponding "job enrichment" for the individual employee (see Kühl 2017a for a critical discussion of flat hierarchies). Against the background of this development, the current prominence of compliance management is all the more surprising.

While modern management concepts advocate above all the reduction of bureaucracy and rigid structures as well as the strengthening of the responsibility of each individual employee, compliance management—not necessarily in its objectives, but in its means—appears as the exact opposite. In order to clearly assign responsibilities in the event of a rule violation, a high level of bureaucratic documentation is often necessary. And instead of strengthening personal responsibility, sophisticated control mechanisms are being devised. We could also say that while agile organizational concepts want to sacrifice formal structure in favor of informality, compliance management aims to push all behavior towards rule conformity and to delegitimize rule deviations as well as informal arrangements.

THEORY

The 'Compliance Culture' Trap

Some organizations identify a need for a "compliance culture" or "integrity management" in order to resolve the dilemma of flexibility and personal responsibility on the one hand and bureaucratization and formalization on the other (Paine 1994). This appeals to the hope that employees will behave more in accordance with the rules if conformity with formal rules is not only formally monitored, but if compliance with the rules is elevated to a central organizational value, which would then also be "lived" in informality. Some assume that, to do this, it would be necessary for compliance with the rules to no longer be perceived as a disruptive burden, but rather as a self-evident premise of one's own daily actions.

On one hand, this is not wrong, but on other hand it overestimates the chances of success of such attempts at value setting, at least when they are supposed not only to be presentable on the display side but also effective in changing the actual behavior (or even consciousness) of the employees.

This is especially the case whenever rule violations occur not because of moral misorientation on the part of employees, but because of tensions within the formal organizational structure (David-Barrett et al. 2017; Pinto et al. 2008) or between the formal organizational structure and practical work requirements. Appeals for morality, ethics or integrity as well as related sensitization training seem to miss the point of the problem. Instead, when looking at a compliance culture, the same thing should apply that applies to all attempts to exert influence on organizational culture: the only available starting point is to change the formal structure and thereby—indirectly—also influence the organizational culture (Kühl 2018).

2.2 The Function of Control Fictions

Such ambitions of total control and formalization fulfill important functions for organizations. However, these lie less in the coordination of organizational internal processes than on the display side of the organization. All companies must maintain a rhetoric of control vis-à-vis their customers, suppliers and competitors, but also towards regulatory authorities and investors, in order to be regarded as a rational and above all reliable partner (Ahrne/Brunsson 2011; Brunsson/Sahlin-Andersson 2000). Nobody likes to do business with someone who is up and down, who does not know who has what competences, or who cannot be relied on to implement agreements.

In addition, legal regulations suggest that organizations cultivate a control rhetoric. This applies in particular with regard to regulations regarding the distribution of responsibilities within the organization, the standardization of (work) processes and products, and the accountability of management. But precisely because experiences of partial coordination failure are commonplace, organizations strive, at least on their display side, to create an image of control and rationality that counteracts the impression of irrationality, a lack of professionalism, and loss of control. Websites and glossy brochures serve as stagings of rationality as well as an adroit style of interaction in external communications (Kette 2018a, 93ff.).

In addition to these display side functions, however, great hopes are often placed on increased control with regard to internal aspects of the organization. In particular, a strict control regime should motivate employees not only to simulate work, but to actually do it in exactly the way the rules dictate. This hope is essentially based on two assumptions: first, that employees make cost-benefit assessments to decide for or against (compliant) work on this basis; and second, that control measures are harmless to the organization itself.

The findings of organizational research give occasion to question and doubt both assumptions. Individual cost-benefit calculations may also play a role in violating organizational rules. An equally important but often overlooked reason for deviating from the rules, however, lies in the organizational structures themselves (Vaughan 1998), whether this is because employees are exposed to contradictory formal expectations, or because an informal culture of deviation has developed. And even the second assumption, according to which control measures are harmless, can hardly stand up in view of the empirical research results available.

Admittedly, control measures can in part strengthen regular discipline and influence the behavior of employees accordingly. Nevertheless, studies show that increased controls and efforts for transparency are also accompanied by dysfunctional effects (Albu/Ringel 2018; Osrecki 2015). Ethan S. Bernstein (2012), for example, has observed how employees set up internal display sides in order to be able to continue to practice informal practices despite increased control efforts. And Frank Anechiarico and James B. Jacobs in their study of the fight against corruption in the public administration of New York City, showed how employees moved discussions of official matters to their private mobile phones because they feared that their office phones were being tapped by compliance employees (Anechiarico/Jacobs 1996, 89f.). Both approaches—the construction and maintenance of internal display sides, and the effort to completely elude control—are costly. They take time and attention. This obviously leads to inefficiencies, and such evasive maneuvers also reinforce the decoupling of actual labor practices from the official rules. So instead of promoting compliance, control ambitions sometimes have the opposite effect: deviant behavior continues to intensify and devours more and more resources. Similar adverse effects are also known from the field of risk management (Pernell et al. 2017).

As functional as the presentation of control ambitions may be on the display side of an organization, these examples already show how momentous and problematic control measures can be in an organization's inner world. This is all the more true when there is a simplified instrumental-rational understanding within the organization of how its own organization works. It is precisely for this reason that it is necessary to ascertain more precisely the limits and potentially dysfunctional effects of controls, rules and sanctions. This, however, requires a more complex conception of organizations than is offered by the instrumental-rational machine model.

> EXAMPLE
>
> **Control Ambitions and Informal Evasions in a Pharmaceutical Company**
>
> This example of a globally active pharmaceutical manufacturer shows how the marketing department was forced to make lateral informal movements in order to ensure the market success of a product. The marketing department wanted to adjust the product's positioning to market conditions and the considerations of the attending physicians. To do this, they wanted to hold an event with physicians in order to find out how they viewed diagnosis and treatment. In order to get a good idea of the physicians' perspectives, the physicians would set discussion topics that would be developed during the event. In addition, doctors would receive a fee for their services.
>
> From a compliance point of view, it is clear that workshop participants could only receive a fee if the event did not serve advertising purposes; otherwise it would be bribery. To ensure the exclusion of advertising content, all content for the event had to be approved by the medical, legal and compliance departments four weeks in advance.

In addition, from a compliance point of view, it was clear that the marketing department could only have a discussion with the physicians within the narrow limits of the approval of the product. Marketing was not supposed to cross this boundary in its interactions with market participants. For the doctors, this separation is artificial. In everyday life, they are constantly confronted with situations in which product approval has to be broadly interpreted for good reasons in order to be able to offer patients any therapy at all. It was clear that the discussion at the event would reflect this.

The marketing department was faced with the challenge of pushing the project into the existing straitjacket of guidelines. Although the marketing department knew that the physicians would discuss beyond the limits of the approval, this part of the discussion was not addressed in writing in the submitted materials. To ensure this, the marketing department entered into a pact with the medical department; they would lead the 'off-topic' discussion on site. The medical department only agreed to this pact because it was in line with the orientation of the workshop.

The approval of the event contents could only be initiated by marketing a good two weeks before the actual date, as only then could the content orientation be discussed with the doctors in advance. To ensure that the process would still work, a fictitious event date was entered in the system in order to have four weeks to go. It was known that the process usually lasted less than two weeks. It was not possible to explicitly request

> this fast-track procedure. Auditing departments would then retreat to formal requirements and work by the rule book to enforce compliance with formal rules.

2.3 The Shortsightedness of Panoptic Control Visions and the Significance of Informal Latitude

The problem with the short-sightedness of panoptic control visions is not that the chances of success of control are overestimated; the problem is the rational understanding of organization, on the basis of which visions of control thrive. This understanding of organizations contains a number of implications that misread the actual challenge in the design of organizational compliance management: maintaining spaces of informality and thus also flexibility.

The idea inherent in compliance management—to delegitimize informality and to dissolve it in favor of formality—would be unproblematic if organizations existed within a completely predictable world. Not only could all conceivable events be anticipated, but, more importantly, all actual events could be anticipated, and for each of these cases organizations could determine precisely how to react. They could also know how these reactions would be reacted to inside and outside the organization, so that clear rules could be formulated for dealing with these reactions, and so on. The organization would never be confronted with surprises and could be set up as a purely formal structure of nested conditional programs.

Unfortunately (or fortunately), the real world doesn't work that way. It is full of minor and major surprises, some of them with far-reaching consequences. Formal decision programs and communication channels therefore only provide a rather abstract orientation that in everyday life, however, must be constantly supplemented by informal agreements and ad hoc communications, or adapted to unexpected circumstances. It is precisely because the formal structure can only prepare for such situations—those that are expected and taken into account during the establishment and design of communication channels and decision programs—that any unexpected event presents itself as a challenge that must be dealt with spontaneously. Formal rules are therefore, inevitably, always incomplete.

In addition to the impossibility of making meaningful arrangements for all conceivable events in advance, there is a second reason why informal deviations from, and additions to, formal requirements occur regularly and necessarily in organizations: formal requirements sometimes contradict practical work requirements (Bensman/Gerver 1963; Kühl 2007). In their environment, organizations face very different expectations from stakeholders. Sometimes organizations take these expectations into account by adapting their display side accordingly, and by setting up their formal structure to accommodate such aspects of legitimacy. However, such requirements are not necessarily efficient, so that they are in fact "overwritten" by deviating informal expectations in everyday working life. And the corresponding expectations cannot always be consistently integrated with each other either. If companies are to produce sustainably and profitably at the same time, the corresponding tensions can often only be resolved by decoupling formal structure from informal practice (Meyer/Rowan 1977).

As a rule, such spontaneous adaptations and deviations from formal rules in organizations are made without a sound. Particularly in the case of minor disturbances, whatever appears to be necessary, depending on the situation, is most often simply done, without having to make an elaborate comparison with all the applicable formal requirements. The extent to which organizations depend on such informal bridging of formalization gaps and sometimes also on the violation of rules—in the sense of "useful illegality" (Luhmann 1964, 304ff.)—becomes obvious when we realize that working by the book is still one of the most effective forms of digging your heels in. The organization then fails, as it were, because of the unavoidable inadequacy of its own formal structures and thus ultimately because of itself.

Taken together, therefore, deviating behavior is by no means primarily due to the opportunistic behavior of individual members of the organization, who are primarily concerned with satisfying their own needs and maximizing their own benefits. Instead, the reasons can be found in contradictory requirements and in the organizational structures themselves. But this also means that it is too short-sighted to view informal practices that deviate from formal rules as evils that must be avoided at all costs. At least in part, informal leeway—even where it violates formal rules—is functional and sometimes even indispensable for organizations.

If we take these insights of a more complex understanding of organization seriously and keep in mind the respective meaning as well as the interaction between the display side, the formal side and the informal side, it becomes clear how tricky and risky the "from now on everything according to the rule book" paradigm of compliance management is. The delegitimization of the informal leads to a complete absence of informal action, which will foreseeably result in "failure according to regulations" and in this sense "useless legality" (Kette 2017). Wherever informal actions are maintained despite the meta-formalization by compliance management, the effort required to hide this will rise predictably. The management challenge in the design of compliance management is therefore not to fall into the "formalization trap," but rather to exploit the potential for flexibility, which also includes the preservation of informal leeway.

EXAMPLE

The Price of Undermining Extensive Rule Books

A large international systems engineering company provides a good example of how internal display sides are elaborately constructed for compliance management when strong regulation forces the renunciation of informal freedoms.

Embezzlement had been going on in the company for several years. When stricter regulations came into force, incidents became public. The company management was forced to clear up the grievances within the company. The compliance department was granted extensive authority to set and monitor regulations. From then on, the compliance department sat at the table at every meeting that could potentially deal with a strategic or organizational realignment of parts of the organization. The result was a comprehensive set of compliance rules.

The employees dedicated themselves meticulously to complying with the comprehensive compliance regulations, not least because the company management had declared that this was a top priority for the boss. At the same time, it became clear that the focus on detailed and bureaucratic conditional programs was swallowing up much of the employees' capacities. This made a customer-oriented approach in an international context considerably more difficult.

This led to latent accusations of bureaucratization, which were received by the compliance department, which then initiated a program to reduce bureaucracy. Employees could now send the compliance department a notice via email if they noticed rules that seemed too complex, conflicted with other objectives, or were broken for these reasons.

The email inbox remained largely empty, although employees became more and more expert at disregarding compliance rules. Some groups had thought things over carefully and had agreed with affected colleagues to disregard rules. No one wanted to draw the compliance department's attention to this under any circumstances. This would have meant losing hard-won informal freedoms and the acceptance of new regulations. There was also the danger that employees or colleagues with whom they had collaborated would have to explain the violation of the rules and endure sanctions. Thus, they paid very meticulous attention to protecting the freedoms gained from monitoring compliance. The display side shown towards compliance was perfected in this way: employees were particularly eager to report compliance in those areas where they felt compliance was less burdensome or counterproductive. This allowed them to prevent the compliance department from becoming too curious about other things.

3. Managing Compliance Management—Approaches to Designing Compliance Management

If work routines function smoothly within organizations, they often do so not *because of* formal decision programs and communication channels, but *despite* the (well-intentioned) formal structure. The basis for success lies more in informal expectations, because they offer much more freedom to react flexibly to *unexpected* situations. This is all the more true in comparison to the strict if-then rules of conditional programs, which define all relevant events (the "if" component) and reactions to them (the "then" component) in advance. This dilemma—in which measures aimed at ensuring compliance with rules simultaneously threaten and restrict the flexibility of specialist departments—is well known in principle. Some of the illuminating contributions to the debate on compliance management therefore point out that the strict formal orientation of compliance management and the delegitimization of informal practices can have dysfunctional consequences for the organization.

The advice often given in this context is that we have to find the right balance. This recommendation, however, merely reformulates the problem. The question of how to find the right balance, and how to tell whether the balance is right, is left open all too often. Furthermore, telling employees in compliance management not to exaggerate would appear to be a paradoxical task. They should ensure compliance with the rules, just not at any price. This would shift the entire burden of the dilemma of simultaneously increasing compliance and flexibility over to compliance management personnel.

In essence, this is a contradictory objective for the compliance department: the effects of one's own decisions will form the foundation of these decisions, but without it being clear whether conformity or flexibility gains will be assigned higher value. The "total regulation" of the organization can therefore hardly be prevented by warning the compliance department to restrain itself. Such an approach only increases the uncertainties for everyone involved.

Instead, we recommend taking this common-sense intention into account when designing compliance management. It is therefore necessary to create framework conditions that prevent the "local rationality" (Cyert/March 1992, 165) of compliance management, with its strict orientation toward rules, from dominating all other local rationalities within the organization. The balance often called for is therefore not a task for compliance management, but, in the best case, the result of a dispute between compliance management and other departments within the organization.

This all begins with the design of formal decision programs and communication channels that are valid for the compliance department itself and thus represent the structural framework for the work in, and decisions by, compliance management. This also shifts the focus of the task at hand, away from "compliance management" to "management of compliance management" and everything that means: namely, away from the rules that are monitored, sanctioned and, if necessary, set anew *by* compliance management, towards those rules that apply *to* compliance management itself when monitoring, sanctioning and developing rules.

Such a *management of compliance management* is interested in the options and respective consequences of the organizational integration of compliance management. The question of how decision programs and communication channels are designed must be clarified with regard to three reference problems: first, with regard to the question of which rules and competencies apply to compliance management in rule monitoring; second, with regard to the rules and competencies applicable to compliance management in the event of sanctioning observed violations; and finally, with regard to the rules and competencies of compliance management in the development of new rules.

THEORY

Organizations as Multi-perspectival Systems— the Concept of Local Rationality

Organizations are horizontally and vertically differentiated systems. They are constituted of different departments, each with different responsibilities, and different hierarchical levels, each with different decision-making competencies. The concept of local rationality reflects the fact that within an organization—depending on the department and/or hierarchy level—different perspectives on the organization and the organizational environment develop. For example, different types of information are considered relevant, problems are interpreted differently and, accordingly, different solution strategies are considered plausible or ineffective. From the R&D department's perspective, for example, a slump in sales can only be reversed by massive expansion in R&D staff counts, whereas the marketing department will be more inclined to plead for an increase in the advertising budget.

All of these perspectives are important for organizations. Organizations cannot thrive without satisfied customers, without an efficient production method, without legally secure contracts, without the development of new products, etc. At the same time, however, the various perspectives cannot easily be reconciled with each other, nor can they always be brought into a valid ranking. On the other hand, this constant competition among perspectives ensures that every perspective wins out sometimes, but no one perspective wins out all the time. The "system rationality" of the organization (Luhmann 1977) lies in this shift in orientation towards different local rationalities.

The organizational structures consisting of communication channels, decision programs and personnel influence local rationalities because they can allocate responsibilities, open up or limit room for maneuver, distribute risks and create incentives. It is precisely for this reason that it is important to take into account the local rationalities of those affected in the context of organizational design, and also in the development of organizational rules.

3.1 Beyond Total Control, or the Art of Avoiding Awareness

The control and monitoring of compliance is at the heart of any compliance management system. If we are interested in how compliance management itself can be managed, this leads to two major design questions. On the one hand, there is the question of the scope of compliance management. This addresses the fact that decision programs can be used to pre-structure which organizational rules are subject to meta-formalization by compliance management. The continuum ranges from a maximum variant, in which all formal rules are monitored by compliance management, to a very minimal variant, in which compliance management is only entrusted with the monitoring of highly sensitive legal aspects.

Anything along this continuum is conceivable. The challenge here is to set up decision programs and communication channels in such a way that they can counteract the trend towards full formalization. If compliance management decides alone and independently on the rules it monitors, it is logical for it to declare itself responsible for as many rules as possible—whether it is to strengthen its own position and relevance within the organization, or to protect itself against possible accusations of omission. One starting point could be to take the question of which rules are subject to monitoring by compliance management off of the compliance management table, or to set up structures in such a way that compliance management has to justify its monitoring claims. Insofar as compliance management bears the responsibility for minimizing legal risks, it will insist on appropriate monitoring in sensitive areas and fight for those mandates. Since such struggles can be very complex under certain circumstances, compliance management will hardly want or be able to wage all of these battles for all organization rules. This shows how the local rationality of compliance management can be influenced through the concrete design of decision programs and communication channels. Depending on who is to be involved in decisions about the responsibility of compliance management, and who has to bear which burden of justification, different alternatives for action in compliance management appear to be plausible and worthwhile.

In addition to the question of *which rules* are subject to monitoring by compliance management, the question of *how* monitoring is structured by compliance management should be at least as relevant. So how is the information generated that compliance management uses as the basis for assessing rules that have been observed or disregarded? Do these occur *en passant*, as it were, for example through digital timestamps, or are they generated in separate work steps by filling out forms with mandatory fields?

EXAMPLE

Restrict or Expand Meta-Formalization?

In the European Union, pharmaceutical companies are legally required to report the side effects of their products. There are clear differences in the ways in which this legal norm is transformed into formal rules by companies and how far the meta-formalization by compliance management reaches, since the legal and compliance departments of the pharmaceutical companies interpret the implementation of this norm differently. Two examples illustrate the consequences of a limited or far-reaching meta-formalization.

In one pharmaceutical company, employees are obliged to do the following: "If you receive reports of side effects of our substances in discussions with doctors, you must immediately forward the information to our internal department to ensure the safety of our substances." Whether employees follow this rule is no longer monitored.

In another pharmaceutical company, the legal and compliance department took a much more regulatory approach. Employees have to use an Intranet tool to report on interactions with doctors on a weekly basis, regardless of whether the contacts had anything to do with side effects. The system also specifies the exact times when employees must report: every Monday about the previous week. An entry is considered delayed if it is made on Wednesday or later. Regardless of the actual reason, employees have to enter the following information: How many doctors were contacted? How many doctors responded? Did you talk about side effects? Have the side effects been reported? Were side effects reported within the specified time?

In this second example, compliance violations often occur because employees do not use the tool until Wednesdays or later. Otherwise, they would have to postpone other work

> in order to complete the entry on time on Mondays. At the same time, it is questionable whether the extensive reporting system will result in better compliance with legal norms than in the first example. To date, neither of the two companies has violated the rule. In the second example, compliance management quite obviously has far-reaching powers to implement meta-formalization. This extensive authority has led so far to more bureaucracy and extensive data collection, but not to more compliance.

In order to keep its own control efforts to a minimum, but also to be able to clearly ascertain who deviates from the rules, the local rationality of compliance management—in the sense of the panoptic control paradigm—initially suggests that efforts should be made to provide information that is as comprehensive and technically generated as possible regarding compliance with the rules. Flexibility and informal latitude can be achieved here if the decision programs and communication channels are designed in such a way that compliance management is 'allowed' to avoid awareness of rule violations.

Depending on how compliance management is integrated into organizational reporting channels, the specialist departments receive more or less autonomy, also with regard to the assessment of and handling of such informal practices that violate formal requirements. For example, a subsidiary principle would be conceivable, according to which the first point of contact for reporting rule violations would be the respective supervisor. The supervisor then decides for himself whether corresponding deviations from the rules are tolerated, internally punished or passed on, be it to the next higher supervisor or to the responsible units in compliance management.

Such a delayed escalation has the advantage of increasing the chances of establishing and using informal leeway within the specialist departments and increasing the corresponding potential for flexibility. In addition, the 'overlooking' of rule violations represents an important exchange good for supervisors in order to be able to motivate temporarily necessary additional services on an informal basis (Gouldner 1964 [1954]). The disadvantage—or better: the consequence—of such an approach is that the supervisor in question must assume responsibility for any breaches of the rules that have not been reported. This shifts the risk of later justifications for such decisions from informally acting employees to lenient supervisors. The latter will therefore likely tolerate informal practices only to the extent that this succeeds in furnishing its decision with "good reasons" in order to protect it against possible future objections and demands.

3.2 Beyond Unconditional Sanctioning, or the Composure to Maintain Informalities

The effects of compliance management on an organization are not limited to the question of how many and which formal expectations are monitored by compliance management. The question of what actually happens after rule-breaking behavior has occurred and been discovered is also at least as important. A second approach to allowing more or less informality and flexibility can therefore be found in the structural design of the sanctioning of rule violations.

The decision programs and communication channels relevant for compliance management can be set up very differently, setting up a continuum between two poles. On the strict side, there are predefined penalty catalogs. In essence, these are conditional programs that provide information on both the causes of sanctions (the "if" condition) and the sanctions to be imposed (the "then" condition). The advantage of such penalty catalogs is that they can contribute to equal treatment of all members. At the same time, however, this is their greatest disadvantage, as they are not sensitive to the contexts and circumstances of the violation. Punishing members whose behavior has violated organizational rules is obvious and sometimes difficult to avoid, either for legal or symbolic reasons. Sometimes, however, it may seem advisable to take into account the circumstances and reasons for a violation when assessing the infringement.

On the other side of the continuum there are procedural decision programs. Instead of specifying which penalty is to be imposed for which offence, such procedural decision programs and communication channels initially only regulate how—i.e. by means of which procedures—a decision is made on the sentencing in the event of a detected breach of the rules. Such procedural rules can then open up leeway in order to take into account the circumstances of the rule violation and, if necessary, even tolerate a 'justified' deviation from the rule. While in the first case the sanctioning follows an automatic process, in this second case the detection of rule violations only leads to the initiation of an internal procedure within the organization in order to decide on the consequences.

The key advantage of such a process-oriented approach is not first and foremost to enable gentler contact with individual organization members, although there may also be advantages to this. The main advantage of such an approach, however, is likely to be that it breaks with the automatic sanction system and thus offers organizations an alternative option for dealing with rule violations. Violations of the rules can be used as an occasion for organizational learning.

Certainly, there are cases of rule violations that are motivated solely by the pursuit of personal advantage. The spectrum of motivations ranges from personal enrichment to making everyday work a little simpler. While cases of personal enrichment are also punishable under criminal law, it is worth taking a more differentiated look at the latter case. One may insist that a rule violation always remains a rule violation. On the other hand, rule violations can also be understood from a non-normative perspective as an indication of a problematic organizational structure. Obviously, the organizational structure is designed in such a way that in certain situations it seems sensible (or even inevitable?) for certain members to behave in violation of the rules. Instead of automatic sanctioning in these cases, it may be better to investigate the question of why compliance with the rules did not seem possible or meaningful.

An opportunity to preserve the informal leeway of specialist departments lies in breaking through the tendency towards meta-formalization and regulation in compliance management, to the effect that the detection of rule deviations is not automatically taken as an occasion for sanctions (Schütz et al. 2018, 166f. also points in this direction). Instead, it may make more sense to question the consequences of informal practices that have been noted. Not every deviation from the rules necessarily leads to harmful effects. Wherever informal rule deviations remain harmless, initiatives for strict rule enforcement seem more risky than do rule deviations.

This becomes clear when we realize that each formal snippet also has unintended effects on both the formal and the informal structure. Strict adherence to a rule that makes sense in itself may not fit seamlessly into other established work processes. Informal practices and rule violations then appear as practices of reducing (unavoidable) tensions in the formal structure. If these are suppressed, it is to be expected that the stress in the network of the formal structure will shift and (new) control deviations will arise elsewhere as a result of informal avoidance strategies.

The existence of these kinds of "new informalities," however, along with their effects, remain unknown until they are discovered. They may worsen the problem that the rule-breaker originally thought they were solving by avoiding original rule violations. In addition, they are likely to create new problems, which remain to be discovered, possibly at a high cost.

In short, if an organization that functions entirely according to the formal rules must remain a panoptic dream anyway, and if the emergence of informal practices is always to be reckoned with in order to compensate for inconsistencies in the formal structure, then an alternative strategy to the automatic sanctioning mechanism is: "Nurture your informalities," meaning, instead of repressing informalities, get to know and understand them.

Even such a strategy has its limits, without question. To be able to consider and apply them at all requires an enlightened understanding of how organizations work. Such an understanding leads to the insight that informalities are simply a part of organizations. Then, however, it is better to deal with known, largely harmless informalities than to constantly generate new, unknown informalities through a self-imposed obligation to sanction. "Nurture your informalities" therefore also means, "Know your organization!"

EXAMPLE

When Quality Assurance Nurtures Its Faults

A manufacturer of food additives had drawn up detailed rules for production. There were rules about which protective clothing had to be worn, which tools could (not) be used and which work steps had to be carried out in which order. The result was long lists of rules for each workstation that all employees could see. These lists were the result of setting a new rule after each detected deviation in order to prevent a further deviation.

One day, the automated optical inspection at the end of the production line discovered that some dosing vials contained small pieces of glass. After several batch checks, it was clear that the optical inspection had identified all contaminated vials. After a long analysis, the 'Quality Assurance Task Force' found that the glass containers had been damaged by the use of cutter knives during the unpacking of production materials. As a result, glass splinters had entered production and were finally found in the filled vials at the end of the production line.

Now there were two ways to deal with this realization. You could set a new rule: "Cutter knives are forbidden in the delivery hall!" This would have required changing other work steps where cutter knives were being used to save time. In addition, the cutter knife might have been used informally in order to comply with production speed specifications.

The other option was not to make a formal change. Finally, the investigations showed that the automated optical inspection system reliably detected all glass pieces. Accordingly, production safety was not restricted at all. In addition, the financial risk of a faulty batch was known and manageable. At the same time, production output seemed to come under greater pressure from a ban on cutter knives in the delivery process, since this would hamper the rapid processing of delivered raw materials.

The company arrived at this conclusion because they understood the (informal) processes of the organizational unit and could foresee the consequences of changes in the processes. After all, it was a question of risk assessment: What (financial) risk would one take if the error were maintained instead of changed? In this example it seemed functional to avoid imposing even tighter regulations, and to tolerate the uncovered error instead.

Admittedly, it is demanding to understand the role of compliance management in this context not exclusively as "organizational police," but to understand rule violations as an opportunity for reflection, which creates an opportunity for the organization to understand its own structures, their effects and thus ultimately itself better.

Above all, this presupposes that the decision premises relevant for compliance management are structurally set up in such a way that sanctioning remains, of course, a possible reaction to breaches of rules, but that the waiver of sanctioning is added as an alternative option. The greatest challenge here is to assess both the consequences and damage potential of deviations from the rules, as well as *compliance* with the rules. In such an expanded understanding of compliance management, particular importance is attached to the decision premise "personnel," who are now required to have skills that extend beyond the knowledge of (legal) rules: namely, they have to understand the effect of rules and the functioning of organizations. This is most likely to succeed if compliance management is not left to *rule experts* alone, but also includes *organizational experts* in the decision-making processes, including in the process of rule development.

3.3 Beyond the Limits of Formalization, or the Danger of Overlooking Organizational Risks

The importance of the organizational experts mentioned above is also particularly clear in the development of new rules or the revision of existing rules. Compliance management's third task is the development of rules, alongside rule monitoring and the sanctioning of rule violations. This is particularly true in the context of organizations that operate in a very dense regulatory environment with numerous and complex regulations, such as those typical for the financial or pharmaceutical industries. Finally, under these circumstances, translation efforts are regularly required in order to transpose amended or newly created legislation into internal organizational rules (Edelman 1992).

We have already seen that the tendency towards meta-formalization is deeply rooted in the concept of compliance management. In organizational reality, this tendency will strengthen itself again insofar as each newly created rule underlines the internal significance of compliance management positions. Precisely because compliance management monitors an important zone of uncertainty for the organization with the interpretation of legal norms, rule development processes offer excellent platforms for compliance management to demonstrate its own relevance.

As a consequence, the development of rules follows an additive logic: new rules will be introduced, but hardly any existing rules will be abolished. Over time, compliance management therefore tends to establish an ever denser network of formal rules, which threatens to further restrict the informal scope and decision-making flexibility of the specialist departments. And also, where rules are revised, this might ultimately result in a more precise definition in the sense that the corresponding rule grows inward, as it were, by introducing more criteria and conditions in order to finally create "clarity" and "perfect" the rule structure in the sense of a machine model.

Accordingly, the challenge in managing compliance management lies less in further specifying formal structures or even in making them more comprehensive. Rather, the problem is precisely the other way round: How can we offset the formalization tendency so that the organization does not become petrified in its own formal structures and their meta-formalization?

When it comes to the development of rules, there are essentially two levers that can be used to promote or curb formalization tendencies. On the one hand, this concerns the question of what circumstances are taken as an occasion for the development of new rules or the revision of existing rules. On the other hand, it must be decided who is to be involved in the process of rule development. Both questions aim at the decision premises of compliance management and therefore come into question as approaches for its design.

In a very minimal and narrow variant, the reasons for rule development may lie solely in changes in the law. In other words, compliance management always deals with the development or revision of rules when the legal situation changes. The other extreme would be to authorize compliance management with an active order to find meta-formalization opportunities. In this variant, there is ultimately no need for a specific reason for rule development, since the development of rules is understood as a permanent task of compliance management.

The probably most radical counter-draft would consist, however, of entrusting compliance management with the elaboration of new rules only if a need for clarification comes from the specialist departments with regard to the interpretation of legal provisions. On the one hand, this would mean reducing compliance management to a kind of internal legal advice for specialist departments, which always reduces uncertainties when *others*—i.e. the respective specialist departments—articulate a corresponding need. This should very effectively prevent over-regulation of the organization. On the other hand, such a reversal of circumstances in practice also means renouncing the advantages of the division of labor. Either the specialist departments themselves become mini-legal experts in such a structure, or, even more likely, both the knowledge and the value of legal regulations will decrease within organizations. Such a variant therefore makes little sense if one wants to establish effective compliance management.

Still, in view of the tendencies towards formalization and the consequences of excessive regulation, it would seem sensible to develop mechanisms that ensure that the development of rules is *quantitatively economical* and *qualitatively prudent*. Quantitative economy means that rules are developed only for those areas in which their need can be justified. Decision programs can distribute the burden of justification accordingly: there is then no need to prove that it would be *possible* without rules; instead, proof must be submitted that it *cannot be done* without rules. Qualitative prudence means estimating and taking into account the organizational consequences of developed rules.

Such qualitative prudence in rule development can be achieved by starting with the decision premise of personnel and filling compliance management positions with organizational experts. It is still a common, or at least widespread, practice to fill compliance management positions with lawyers. In view of the fact that rules formulated in compliance management and practices to be evaluated often refer to legal texts, this is comprehensible and plausible. However, it is precisely when there is no direct and close legal link that it may make sense to supplement the strict regulatory perspective with a reflective organizational perspective in order to be able to incorporate the effects of a restrictive regulatory policy into the decision-making process. And with regard to the implementation of legal requirements, in most cases they must be interpreted because they are not entirely clear (Bergmann 2016; Edelman/Talesh 2011). However, this need for interpretation is also an opportunity for design; the fact that it is not clear how a legal regulation is to be implemented, precisely and in detail, opens up room for maneuver in which different variants can be considered. Such a broadening of perspective may counteract the danger that attempts to avert legal risks not only create organizational risks, but also leave them undiscovered.

The feasibility of this strategy will also be subject to restrictions here and there. Where compliance management 'merely' consists of the role of *a* 'representative,' it will hardly be possible to hire a lawyer *and* an organizational expert. On the one hand, however, such a 'weak' compliance management might only have limited influence anyway, which gives the problems described here a bit more urgency. On the other hand, thinking about "organizational experts" may also be helpful when selecting a Compliance Management Officer to identify suitable candidates. For larger compliance management departments, on the other hand, it makes sense to consider setting up positions for organizational experts, whether they are sociologists of organizations or lawyers trained in organizational sociology.

4. Conclusion—
Discursive Compliance Management

Compliance management is based on the idea of a control program to prevent behavior that deviates from the rules. The background assumption is that organizational rule violations are accompanied by legal and reputational risks, and that these risks can be avoided or at least reduced through control measures. As we have seen, however, deviations from the rules sometimes also fulfill important functions in organizations. They allow you to handle conflicting requirements and react flexibly to unforeseen situations. Against this background, however, it is important to note that attempts to achieve full compliance with the rules entail considerable organizational risks.

The consequence of this realization is not to diminish the importance of organizational compliance management, but rather to underline the magnitude of the challenge. Finally, it is hardly possible for compliance management to accept the violation of formal rules, since compliance, by definition, is aimed at compliance with the formal structure. When designing an organizationally intelligent compliance management, it is important to proceed in a reflective manner and to develop concepts for dealing with informality. And that means designing the decision programs and communication channels of compliance management in a way that takes into account the perspective of those actors who are to comply with the formal rules.

In essence, these considerations lead to a common focus. The main problem in connection with compliance management procedures is that both the methods of rule monitoring and the rules produced by compliance management are often difficult to reconcile with, or even contradict, the local rationalities of the departments to be regulated. However, rules that are completely ignorant of the local rationalities of the specialist department affected by them will tend to lead to the construction or extension of facades and display sides within the organization, rather than ensuring that behavior is actually in line with the rules. The specialist departments may then ensure that their activities look compliant. However, their actual actions will often only be loosely oriented towards this, especially if one has good arguments for the alternative interpretation of the formal structures in the event that deviations from the rules are uncovered. For the organization as a whole, inefficiencies arise above all because the construction of display sides costs time and energy, but at the same time the legal and reputational risks for the organization continue to exist. In the context of rules that are of little relevance to the organizational environment, this may not be a major problem. If, however, it is important for risk avoidance that the specialist departments actually act in accordance with the rules, such an ignorant handling of the local rationalities of the "regulated" parties by compliance management appears risky.

The question is therefore always: What do the (new) rules and respective monitoring formats do with the rest of the organization? This question can be entertained by compliance management only very conditionally, since compliance management must insist on rule compliance. Especially with regard to the design of rules, there is, however, room for maneuver which is worthwhile to use. Accordingly, it is advisable to invest in particular in the design of rules.

Most rules in organizations are contingent in the sense that they cannot be formulated arbitrarily but can be formulated in different ways. The challenge is to design a formal rule that is as compatible as possible with the work routines and local rationalities of the departments concerned: The best rule is a rule that can be kept! Of course, this is only possible to the extent that it is possible to take into account local rationalities and the actual practices of the specialist departments in the process of rule formulation. This task is not trivial because neither the local rationalities nor the informal work processes can be directly observed or queried. This requires a discursive approach that invites participation from those being regulated in the specialist departments so that they can be involved in shaping the rules. Within the framework of individual discussions and in work units with a group of actors, it will be possible to approach the formal and, above all, informal practices of the specialist departments and to think about the local rationality of the actors to be regulated.

The involvement of specialist departments does not at all mean letting the fox guard the henhouse. Admittedly, the sensitivity for compliance with formal rules and for possible consequences of a rule violation in the area of sales or R&D per se may not be a focal point of their work. They do whatever promises sales or development progress. However, it is important to understand that compliance management has a high sensitivity for the relevance of formal rules, but that the effects of these rules on sales development and development progress are not equally prominent. Like every department, Compliance Management also has its own specific perspective: create and monitor formal rules to minimize non-compliance and the associated risks to the business. This orientation tends—like the respective orientation of every other department—towards totalization. The one and only thing that is important is sales proceeds, or progress in development, or compliance with rules. On the one hand, the strength of organizations lies in this form of division of labor. When a department focuses on one (or very few) aspects of a problem, then it is relieved of all the other aspects of the problem. On the other hand, *all* orientations are equally important for organizations, since they require sales revenues *and* development progress *and* compliance with rules. This is precisely why no one orientation should permanently dominate all others, not even that of compliance management.

The only way to prevent excessive dominance by one department is to contain it structurally. And that means creating the formal structure in such a way that the departments are confronted with the conflicts of goals within the organization—selectively, but periodically. The management of compliance management aims at such containment, which prevents compliance management within an organization from becoming either extremely weak or extremely powerful. Weak compliance management has so little competence and influence that it does not disturb operational procedures, but also has no effect on conformity with the rules. Ultimately, it has a purely display side function. Powerful compliance management, on the other hand, threatens to overrun the organization with rules, so that flexible action becomes possible only with great effort. This initial situation gives rise to calls for balanced compliance management, which presuppose a degree of self-restraint, reflection and organizational knowledge, but which overtaxes compliance management itself.

We therefore need communication channels and decision programs related to compliance management that are designed in such a way that an organization-conscious discursive exchange arises, in which organizational conflicts of goals can be discussed and negotiated. It is difficult to give a general answer to what is meant by organizational wisdom in detail and it must therefore be worked out individually for each organization. In any case, however, it will be a matter of confronting the perspectives of compliance management and specialist departments with each other. In this process, compliance management can formulate a *regulatory intention* that makes clear which regulatory effects must be achieved by a questionable rule in order to avert or minimize legal risks. In a dispute between the compliance department and the respective specialist departments, it is then a matter of thinking through various *design ideas* and considering their consequences, both with regard to their compatibility with other formal expectations, but also with regard to compatibility with informal practices. Openness to structural alternatives may be limited by certain legal risks. In order to explore these boundaries and mediate between conformity and flexibility requirements, the communication channels and decision programs must be set up in such a way that internal organizational arenas emerge in which the specialist departments and compliance management struggle to derive rules from their local rationalities.

In designing such arenas, the following questions may be helpful: When and under what conditions should the arena be used to negotiate a conflict of objectives? Should the development and change of compliance rules be negotiated in the arena, or should sanctions be imposed in the event of rule violations? The use of the arena could be limited to those areas of business activity where the highest risk of external sanctions exists. In addition, we must also consider which actors or departments should be involved in the development, change and monitoring of compliance rules as well as in the decision on possible sanctions, and which should not.

Our suggestion of an organizationally shrewd formalization and discursive rule development along different local rationalities leads to a mutual limitation of too much or too little influence of compliance management in rule development and change, as well as rule monitoring and sanctioning. The rules of the game are determined by the arenas of conflict negotiation. These rules of the game are clever when they are individually tailored to the organization and think about how actors will stand up for their interests outside these rules. This procedure is obviously a challenge for compliance management insofar as it removes the process of rule design and, in part, limits or removes the evaluation of rule violations from the compliance department's sphere of influence. However, it has the advantage of taking organizations seriously in their complexity and specific functional logic, thus getting compliance management out of the realm of control dreams and making it realistic and applicable.

Bibliography

Ahrne, Göran, and Nils Brunsson. 2011. "Organization Outside Organizations: The Significance of Partial Organization." *Organization* 18: 83–104.

Albu, Oana B., and Leopold Ringel. 2018. "The Perils of Organizational Transparency: Consistency, Surveillance, and Authority Negotiations." In *Toward Permeable Boundaries of Organizations?*, published by Leopold Ringel, Petra Hiller, und Charlene Zietsma, 227-256. Bingley: Emerald Publishing.

Anechiarico, Frank, and James B. Jacobs. 1996. *The Pursuit of Absolute Integrity: How Corruption Control Makes Government Ineffective*. Chicago: University of Chicago Press.

Barreveld, Dirk J. 2002. *The ENRON Collapse: Creative Accounting, Wrong Economics or Criminal Acts?*. San Jose: Writers Club Press.

Bensman, Joseph, and Israel Gerver. 1963. "Crime and Punishment in the Factory: The Function of Deviancy in Maintaining the Social System." *American Sociological Review* 28: 588–598.

Bentham, Jeremy. 2017. *Panopticon: Or the Inspection House*. Whithorn: Anodos Books.

Bergmann, Jens. 2016. "When Compliance Fails." *Compliance Elliance Journal* 2: 85–94.

Bernstein, Ethan S. 2012. "The Transparency Paradox: A Role for Privacy in Organizational Learning and Operational Control." *Administrative Science Quarterly* 57: 181–216.

Brunsson, Nils. 1989. *The Organization of Hypocrisy: Talk, Decisions and Actions in Organizations*. Chichester: Copenhagen Business School Press.

Brunsson, Nils, and Kerstin Sahlin-Andersson. 2000. "Constructing Organizations: The Example of Public Sector Reform." *Organization Studies* 21: 721–746.

Cyert, Richard, and James G. March. 1992. *A Behavioral Theory of the Firm*. Malden, Mass.: Blackwell.

Daft, Richard L., and Karl E. Weick. 1984. "Toward a Model of Organizations as Interpretation Systems." *Academy of Management Review* 9: 284–295.

David-Barrett, Elisabeth, Basak Yakis-Douglas, Amanda Moss-Cowan, and Yen Nguyen. 2017. "A Bitter Pill? Institutional Corruption and the Challenge of Antibribery Compliance in the Pharmaceutical Sector." *Journal of Management Inquiry* 26 (3): 326–347.

Edelman, Lauren B. 1992. "Legal Ambiguity and Symbolic Structures: Organizational Mediation of Civil Rights Law." *American Journal of Sociology* 97 (6): 1531–1576.

Edelman, Lauren B., and Shauhin A. Talesh. 2011. "To Comply or Not to Comply—That Isn't the Question: How Organizations Construct the Meaning of Compliance." In *Explaining Compliance: Business Responses to Regulation*, published by Christine Parker und Vibeke Lehmann Nielsen, 103-122. Northampton, Mass.: Edward Elgar Pub.

Foucault, Michel. 1979. *Discipline and Punish: The Birth of the Prison*. Harmondsworth: Penguin Books.

Fusaro, Peter C., and Ross M. Miller. 2002. *What Went Wrong at Enron: Everyone's Guide to the Largest Bankruptcy in U.S. History*. New York: John Wiley & Sons.

Gouldner, Alvin W. 1964 [1954]. *Patterns of Industrial Bureaucracy: A Case Study of Modern Factory Administration*. New York: Free Press.

Hasse, Raimund, and Klaus P. Japp. 1997. "Dynamik symbolischer Organisationspolitik: Umwelt- und Selbstanpassung als Folgewirkung ökologischer Leistungserwartungen." In *Handbuch Umweltschutz und Organisation: Ökologisierung, Organisationswandel, Mikropolitik*, published by Martin Birke, Carlo Burschel and Michael Schwarz, 134-162. München/Wien: Oldenbourg Verlag.

Heckscher, Charles C., and Anne Donnellon. 1994. *The Post-Bureaucratic Organization: New Perspectives on Organizational Change*. Thousand Oaks: Sage.

International Organization for Standardization (ISO). 2014. *ISO 19600:2014: Compliance Management Systems: Guidelines*. Genf: Selbstverlag.

Kette, Sven. 2017. *Vertrauen ist gut, Kontrolle ist besser? Dysfunktionen organizationalen Compliance-Managements*. Unpublished manuscripts: Luzern.

Kette, Sven. 2018a. *Unternehmen: Eine sehr kurze Einführung*. Wiesbaden: Springer VS.

Kette, Sven. 2018b. "Unsichere Verantwortungszurechnungen: Dynamiken organizationalen Compliance Managements." *GesundheitsRecht* 17 (1): 3–6.

Kette, Sven. 2019. "From Topic to Problem: Organisational Mechanisms of Constructing Demographic Change." In *Studies in the Sociology of Population: International Perspectives*, published by Jon Anson, Walter Bartl and Andrzej Kulczycki, 225-250. Cham: Springer.

Kühl, Stefan. 2007. "Formalität, Informalität und Illegalität in der Organisationsberatung: Systemtheoretische Analyse eines Beratungsprozesses." *Soziale Welt* 58: 271–293.

Kühl, Stefan. 2013. *Organizations: A Systems Approach*. Farnham: Gower.

Kühl, Stefan. 2015. "Gruppen, Organisationen, Familien und Bewegungen: Zur Soziologie mitgliedschaftsbasierter Systeme zwischen Interaktion und Gesellschaft." In *Interaktion—Organisation—Gesellschaft revisited: Anwendungen, Erweiterungen, Alternativen: Sonderheft der Zeitschrift für Soziologie*, published by Bettina Heintz and Hartmann Tyrell, 65-85 Stuttgart: Lucius & Lucius.

Kühl, Stefan. 2017a. *When the Monkeys Run the Zoo: The Pitfalls of Flat Hierarchies*. Princeton: Organizational Dialogue Press.

Kühl, Stefan. 2017b. *Exploring Markets: A Very Brief Introduction*. Princeton: Organizational Dialogue Press.

Kühl, Stefan. 2018. *Influencing Organizational Culture: A Brief Introduction*. Princeton: Organizational Dialogue Press.

Kühl, Stefan, and Judith Muster. 2018. *Designing Organizations: A Very Brief Introduction*. Princeton: Organizational Dialogue Press.

Luhmann, Niklas. 1964. *Funktionen und Folgen formaler Organisation*. Berlin: Duncker & Humblot.

Luhmann, Niklas. 1977. *Zweckbegriff und Systemrationalität: Über die Funktion von Zwecken in sozialen Systemen*. Frankfurt a. M.: Suhrkamp.

Luhmann, Niklas. 2009. "Allgemeine Theorie organisierter Sozialsysteme." In *Soziologische Aufklärung 2: Aufsätze zur Theorie der Gesellschaft*, published by Niklas Luhmann, 48-62. Wiesbaden: VS Verlag für Sozialwissenschaften.

Luhmann, Niklas. 2018. *Organization and Decision*. Cambridge, United Kingdom/New York, NY: Cambridge University Press.

MacLean, Tammy L., and Michael Behnam. 2010. "The Dangers of Decoupling: The Relationship Between Compliance Programs, Legitimacy Perceptions, and Institutionalized Misconduct." *Academy of Management Journal* 53 (6): 1499–1520.

March, James G. 1994. *A Primer on Decision Making: How Decisions Happen*. New York: Free Press.

Mayo, Elton. 1966 [1933]. *The Human Problems of an Industrial Civilization*. 5th ed. London: Routledge & Paul.

Meyer, John W., and Brian Rowan. 1977. "Institutionalized Organizations: Formal Structure as Myth and Ceremony." *American Journal of Sociology* 83: 340–363.

Nelson, J. S. 2017. "The Corruption Norm." *Journal of Management Inquiry* 26 (3): 280–286.

Osrecki, Fran. 2015. "Fighting Corruption with Transparent Organizations: Anti-Corruption and Functional Deviance in Organizational Behavior." *ephemera* 15: 337–364.

Paine, Lynn S. 1994. "Managing for Organizational Integrity." *Harvard Business Review* 72: 106–117.

Pernell, Kim, Jiwook Jung, and Frank Dobbin. 2017. "The Hazards of Expert Control: Chief Risk Officers and Risky Derivatives." *American Sociological Review* 82 (3): 511–541.

Pinto, Jonathan, Carrie R. Leana, and Frits K. Pil. 2008. "Corrupt Organizations or Organizations of Corrupt Individuals? Two Types of Organizational-Level Corruption." *Academy of Management Review* 33: 685–709.

Robertson, Brian J. 2015. *Holacracy: The Revolutionary Management System That Abolishes Hierarchy*. London: Penguin.

Roethlisberger, Fritz J., Williams J. Dickson, and Harold A. Wright. 1967 [1939]. *Management and the Worker: An Account of a Research Program Conducted by the Western Electric Company, Hawthorne Works, Chicago*. Cambridge, Mass.: Harvard University Press.

Salter, Malcom S. 2008. *Innovation Corrupted: The Origins and Legacy of Enron's Collapse*. Cambridge, Mass.: Harvard University Press.

Schütz, Marcel, Richard Beckmann, and Heinke Röbken. 2018. *Compliance-Kontrolle in Organisationen: Soziologische, juristische und ökonomische Aspekte*. Wiesbaden: Springer Gabler.

Silverman, Michael G. 2008. *Compliance Management for Public, Private, or Nonprofit Organizations*. New York: McGraw-Hill.

Singh, Nitish, and Thomas J. Bussen. 2015. *Compliance Management: A How-To Guide for Executives, Lawyers, and Other Compliance Professionals. Santa Barbara*, California: Praeger.

Steinberg, Richard M. 2011. *Governance, Risk Management, and Compliance: It Can't Happen to Us: Avoiding Corporate Disaster While Driving Success*. Hoboken, N.J.: J. Wiley & Sons.

Suchman, Mark C. 1995. "Managing Legitimacy: Strategic and Institutional Approaches." *Academy of Management Review* 20: 571–610.

Taylor, Frederick Winslow. 1967. *The Principles of Scientific Management*. New York: Norton.

Vaughan, Diane 1998. "Rational Choice, Situated Action, and the Social Control of Organizations." *Law and Society Review* 32: 23–61.

Weber, Max. 2009 [1972]. *Wirtschaft und Gesellschaft: Grundriss der verstehenden Soziologie*. Tübingen: Mohr-Siebeck.

Weick, Karl E., Kathleen M. Sutcliffe, and David Obstfeld. 2005. "Organizing and the Process of Sensemaking." *Organization Science* 16: 409–421.

Weidenfeld, Ursula, publisher. 2011. *Nützliche Aufwendungen?: Der Fall Siemens und die Lehren für das Unternehmen, die Industrie und Gesellschaft.* München: Piper.

www.ingramcontent.com/pod-product-compliance
Lightning Source LLC
Chambersburg PA
CBHW020302030426
42336CB00010B/876